NAPLES &
MARCO ISLAND
The Cubby
2024 Long Weekend Guide

James Cubby

NO BUSINESS HAS PAID A SINGLE PENNY OR GIVEN _ANYTHING_ TO BE INCLUDED IN THIS BOOK.

NAPLES & MARCO ISLAND
The Cubby
Long Weekend Guide

TABLES OF CONTENTS

WHY NAPLES & MARCO ISLAND?

A lot of my friends who live in Miami, harried by the unrelenting pace of South Beach, escape along the Tamiami Trail for the completely foreign world that lies two hours away in the laid-back town of Naples.

Naples offers a thoroughly different "escape" from the rigorous pace of Miami that the Florida Keys do not. You can take your flip-flops to the Keys, and you can take your flip-flops to Naples. The difference is one of tone. You won't find a Gucci store in Key West, however. You won't find a cluster of world-class spas either. And won't find a Ritz-Carlton that's rated among the best in the world.

There's a lot of money in Naples. It's the money of Midwesterners who disdain the Miami lifestyle.

This is an unabashedly American city whereas Miami
long ago ceased to have much in common with
America besides its money-laundered currency. The
money in Naples is unostentatiously evident in the
low-level lifestyle than in the crass and glitzy
environs you find in Miami. Among the many who
love Naples, it's a perfect world.
Oh, when you're in Italy, don't call Naples Naples. In
Italy they call it Napoli. I heard a tour guide once say,
"There's no Naples here, it's in Florida."
    And so it is.

MARCO ISLAND

As the largest and northernmost of the Ten Thousand Islands, Marco Island clings like a barnacle to its fishing roots. Marinas on the north end offer everything from fishing charters and boat rentals to sailing excursions and luncheon cruises. It's about a 2-hour drive from Miami on US 41 (the famed Tamiami Trail) or from Fort Lauderdale on I-75.

Visitor Information:

Greater Naples Marco Everglades Convention & Visitors Bureau

239-252-2384 or 800-688-3600

www.paradisecoast.com

GETTING ABOUT

The airport (Southwest Florida International Airport, to be exact) serving Naples is whopping 42 miles from the city, so unless you plan on barely leaving your lodgings during your trip, you're looking at a car rental whether you like it or not.

If, however, you plan on focusing your visit in the Old Town, you can do quite handsomely simply by renting a bike.

BIG MOMMA'S BICYCLES
850 Seagate Dr., Suite F, Naples: 239-263-0728
www.bigmommasbicycles.com

HOTEL

WHERE TO STAY

I always like to offer a choice for those with different budgets. I make three trips to any given destination so your own weekend will be not only memorable, but within your budget.

BELLASERA RESORT LUXURY HOTEL
221 Ninth Street South, Naples: 833-735-0289
www.bellaseranaples.com
Right in the middle of the Old Town you'll find this 4-diamond luxury hotel. Has studios as well as 3-room suites with fully appointed kitchens.

HAWTHORN SUITES NAPLES

3557 Pine Ridge Rd, Naples, 239-593-1300
www.hawthornnaples.com
Nothing fancy, just basic.

HILTON MARCO ISLAND BEACH RESORT

560 S Collier Blvd, Marco Island, 239-394-5000
www.hiltonmarcoisland.com
AAA 4-diamond resort, located off the south coast of
Florida, with nearly 300 luxurious rooms that include
balconies with full or partial views of the beach.
Amenities include a heated outdoor pool, a variety of
water sports, a spa offering a variety of treatments,
three restaurants, two tennis courts and a fitness
center. A variety of tours available including the
10,000 Islands Guided Waverunner Tour.

HYATT HOUSE NAPLES / 5TH AVENUE
1345 5th Avenue South, Naples, 239-775-1000
https://www.hyatt.com/en-US/hotel/florida/hyatt-
house-naples-5th-avenue/napxn
NEIGHBORHOOD: Downtown
Overlooking the Gordon River, this somewhat boring
83-room hotel features modern studios and 1- and 2-
bedroom suites. When booking, be sure you get a
view of the river and the little marinas laid out below
the balconies. Otherwise, you're just in another Hyatt
with nothing really to distinguish it. Amenities:
Complimentary Wi-Fi, satellite TVs, hot breakfast
buffet and furnished balconies. Hotel features: 24/7
Fitness center, laundry facilities, pool, and on-site
restaurant. Pet friendly (surcharge). Conveniently
located near attractions like the Naples Zoo and
Naples Pier. Smoke-free hotel.

THE INN ON FIFTH
699 5th Ave. S., Naples: 239-403-8777
www.innonfifth.com
This smallish property with about 90 rooms is right in
the heart of the city on happening Fifth Avenue
South.

LA PLAYA
9891 Gulf Shore Dr., Naples: 239-597-3123
www.laplayaresort.com
No other hotel has the same immediate access to the
beach than La Playa. It's as good as the Ritz, but not
quite as elegant. Much more intimate. Voted 12th best
resort in the U.S. by Condé Nast readers. Golf, Spa.

MARCO BEACH OCEAN RESORT

480 S Collier Blvd, Marco Island, 239-235-9035
https://www.marcobeachocean.com/
AAA 4-diamond resort with 98 one- and two-bedroom suites with fully equipped kitchens, all facing the gulf. Guests enter a beautiful Mediterranean-styled lobby. Amenities include swimming pool and pool bar located on the fifth-floor rooftop, a spa, fitness center, rooftop gardens, casual resort dining and four miles of white sand beach.

MARCO ISLAND MARRIOTT RESORT & SPA

400 S Collier Blvd, Marco Island, 239-394-2511
www.marcoislandmarriott.com
This world-class resort, set on three miles of beautiful beachfront property, features eight restaurants, oversized rooms, a luxurious spa with Balinese-influenced treatments, two private 18-hole golf courses, and premier amenities. Guests can enjoy a variety of water sports, parasailing, shelling cruises

and sightseeing tours. Located just miles from Naples and Fort Myers.

NAPLES BAY RESORT
1500 5th Ave. S., Naples: 239-530-1199
www.naplesbayresort.com
In the Old Town, this place has a lot to recommend it. It's next to the shopping on Fifth Avenue, has 6 tennis courts, cottages, marina, a yacht club, a spa and it's still reasonably priced.

OLDE MARCO ISLAND INN & SUITES
100 Palm St, Marco Island: 239-394-3131 or 877-475-3466
www.oldemarcoinn.com
Historic Inn feature 50-plus modern one- and two-bedroom suites. The original 1880s inn now houses Bistro Soleil, an elegant restaurant that serves fine French cuisine courtesy of Chef Denis Meurgue.

Amenities include free HBO, Patio gardens, heated pool, and hot tub.

THE RITZ CARLTON
280 Vanderbilt Beach Rd., Naples: 239-598-3300
www.ritzcarlton.com
Hard to beat this place for the ultimate in luxurious lodgings. The **Sand Bar** is actually my favorite thing about this hotel. It's a little bar down by the beach where you feel like you're a million miles from anywhere. To create that illusion when you're really at the edge of one of the best resorts in the world is pretty amazing, but they manage to do it here. Another beachside spot that serves food is **Gumbo Limbo** just a few feet away. It's a bit larger, serves tropically inspired food and shares the breathtaking views of the Gulf. Even if you're not staying at the RC, meander around this property to have a look at how the other half live. Stop by one of these two places for a bite or a drink just to experience the feel

of the hotel voted 9th best hotel in the U.S. by readers of "Travel & Leisure" in 2011. Also a Forbes 4 star property and 5 Diamond. And if you're into pampering, and can afford it, the three-floor Spa here was voted best in Florida by readers of "Spa" magazine.

WHERE TO EAT

ARTURO'S BISTRO
918 N Collier Blvd, Marco Island, 239-394-7578
https://www.arturosbistro.com/
CUISINE: Italian/Seafood
DRINKS: Wine & Beer
SERVING: Dinner (Closed Sundays)
PRICE RANGE: $$
A somewhat upscale eatery (for this part of Florida) offering a menu of Italian classics and seafood favorites. There are a couple of tables outside if you can grab one of them on a night when the weather's

pleasant. Inside, it's a fairly simple affair, but they have little flourishes like the napkins stuffed into the blue water goblets and when they lower the lights in the evening, it gets downright romantic. Menu picks: Not too many surprises on the menu which leans toward traditional Italian favorites. But I always get the Soft Shell Crab Francaise when they have it. It's the same garlic butter with lemon you get on the Veal Picatta or the Chicken Picatta, but with the crabs, they melt in your mouth; otherwise, opt for the succulent Rack of Lamb or the nicely prepared Frog Legs. Delicious soups and salads, one of which you get with your meal.

CAMPIELLO
1177 3rd St S, Naples, 239-435-1166
https://campiellonaples.com/
CUISINE: Italian
DRINKS: Full Bar
SERVING: Lunch & Dinner
PRICE RANGE: $$$
Upscale landmark eatery popular with locals and tourists serving top-notch Italian fare. It's a big modern room with lots of outside patio seating. My Favorites: I love the Beef Short Ribs or I get the Red Snapper sauteed Piccata style. If I opt for one of the succulent homemade pastas, I generally get the Pappardelle with Braised Veal, tomato & oregano— it's a heavenly mixture of savory flavors. Impressive wine list. Reservations recommended.

CAPRI FISH HOUSE RESTAURANT
203 Capri Blvd, Naples, 239-389-5555
www.caprifishhouse.com
CUISINE: Seafood
DRINKS: Full Bar
SERVING: Lunch & Dinner
PRICE RANGE: $$
Casual seafood eatery that offers a creative menu of
tasty treats like alligator nuggets and Salmon Nadine.
Indoor and outdoor dining. Occasional live music.
Great spot to watch the sunset.

CITY SEAFOOD
702 Begonia St, Everglades City, 239-695-4700
http://www.cityseafood1.com/
CUISINE: Seafood/Seafood Market
DRINKS: Beer & Wine
SERVING: 6 a.m. – 6 p.m.
PRICE RANGE: $$
NEIGHBORHOOD: Everglades City
I know this is WAY out of town, but if you're driving
from one coast to the other, you might want to detour
to have lunch or dinner at this great waterside eatery
and seafood market. It's a throwback to those old fish
shacks you used to see all over this part of Florida
decades ago. (I'm old enough to remember, LOL.)
Just a beat-up old wood-planked building that looks
like it needs a paint job, but it's right on the water,
and it couldn't be better if it tried. Great selection of
seafood including crab, frog legs and alligator.
Favorites: Buffalo shrimp wrap and Stone Crabs.
Outdoor seating. Order and wait for your number to
be called over the loudspeaker. See what I said,
nothing fancy.

DA VINCI'S

599 S Collier Blvd, Marco Island, 239-389-1888
https://ristorantedavinci.com/
CUISINE: Italian/Pizza
DRINKS: Full Bar
SERVING: Dinner
PRICE RANGE: $$
Family-owned Italian eatery serving up homemade
sauces and pastas in a room that would be quite plain
if it didn't have the dark wood coffered ceiling which
lends it a little coziness. Favorites: I tend to get the
Eggplant Rollatini to start. Their pastas are all so
good, it's tough to decide, gut I generally end up with
the Cavatelli with broccoli rabe & Italian sausage or
the Tortellini Di Carne. They have a "build your own
pizza"-option if you're into pizza. (I never was,
except for deep-dish.) Excellent tiramisu.

DOCK AT CRAYTON COVE
845 12th Ave S, Naples, 239-263-9940
http://www.dockcraytoncove.com/
CUISINE: Seafood/American (Traditional)
DRINKS: Full Bar
SERVING: Lunch, & Dinner
PRICE RANGE: $$
NEIGHBORHOOD: Old Naples
Dockside eatery overlooking a vast water expanse
and a marina, so you'll want to sit outside if you can.
I love this place when a storm passes by—you see the
dark clouds forming in the sky over the ocean or the
Everglades. You watch them approach and then get
the sound of the rain when it starts. Very nice. Also, a
good spot at sunset. Rustic interior. Has a menu of
seafood and American fare. Nice raw bar selection.
Menu picks: Blackened Mahi Fish Tacos, the
excellent Lobster and the Crab Stuffed Grouper.
Sunday brunch with a make-your-own Bloody Mary
bar. Vegan options.

View from Dolphin Tiki Bar

DOLPHIN TIKI BAR & GRILL

1021 Anglers Cove, Marco Island, 239-394-4048
http://dolphintikibar.com/
CUISINE: Seafood/Sandwiches
DRINKS: Full Bar
SERVING: Lunch & Dinner
PRICE RANGE: $$$

Waterside bar & grill featuring a menu of seafood-focused dishes overlooking the Marco River and the boats lined up on a pier. Variety of sandwiches and appetizers. Favorites: Blackened Shrimp & Scallops and Grouper Tacos. Impressive cocktail menu including specialty frozen drinks. A good place to spend happy hour. It's a little tricky to find, so give yourself plenty of time to get there.

FIN BISTRO

657 S Collier Blvd, Marco Island, 239-970-6064
https://finbistro.com/
CUISINE: Seafood
DRINKS: Full Bar
SERVING: Dinner (Closed Sundays & Mondays)
PRICE RANGE: $$$

A family-run unpretentious seafood eatery with nothing much to recommend it in the "ambience" department. You might ask - Why come here at all? Because the menu showcases a variety of freshly caught seafood, that's the only reason. From flounder (sautéed almond crusted) to the panko crusted snapper to the coconut crusted Key Largo dorado, or the swordfish piccata, it's the fish that makes you want to come back. My special favorite is the Shellfish Meyer Lemon Brodetto, a heady Cioppino style stew that includes clams, rock shrimp, calamari, scallops, all in a white wine tomato lemon broth.

Comes with a corn risotto cake. Their nice wine selection is not overpriced.

GROUPER & CHIPS
338 9th St N, Naples, 239-643-4577
http://www.grouperandchipsnaples.com/
CUISINE: Seafood
DRINKS: Beer & Wine
SERVING: Lunch & Dinner (Closed Sundays)
PRICE RANGE: $$
Tiny no-frills (and I mean no-frills) fish 'n' chips storefront offering a variety of seafood dishes, with a

big emphasis on grouper. I would normally say if you are wary of fried food, stay away, but they actually have a lot of food that's not fried. Almost all their fish can be ordered fried, blackened, sauteed or broiled, but whenever I'm here, all the fat people around me are eating fried food. I get my seafood sauteed in this place. Favorites: Chicken Milanese and Yellowtail Snapper Piccata. Children's menu available.

HOGFISH HARRY'S RESTAURANT & BAR

600 Neapolitan Way, Naples, 239-776-7623
https://hogfishharrys.com/
CUISINE: Seafood
DRINKS: Full Bar
SERVING: Lunch & Dinner
PRICE RANGE: $$$

Upscale seafood eatery with indoor and outdoor seating. This is a such a nice place, made more appealing by its bright blue color scheme. There's lovely outdoor seating on a verandah style porch. Inside, the soaring A-frame ceiling painted bright blue is cheerful & welcoming. My favorites are the Shrimp & Lobster Mac & Cheese (which I share with someone, it's so rich) and the Crispy Hogfish Sandwich that comes with a Mango Jalapeno Remoulade that's to die for. Don't overlook the cheeseburger here because it's so rich and juicy, made with a Brisket Short Rib Blend and has a smoked bacon shallot jam that takes this burger to a higher level. (Oh, and they have a lovely Pineapple Upside Down Cake for dessert that's always good.) Everything cooked from scratch. Impressive wine list.

JIMMY P'S CHARRED
1833 Tamiami Trail North, Naples, 239-643-2427
https://www.jimmypscharred.com/
CUISINE: Butcher Shop/Steakhouse
DRINKS: Beer & Wine
SERVING: Lunch & Dinner
PRICE RANGE: $$

Located in a one of the less-than-glamorous strip-malls that populate the area, this simple & friendly eatery/butcher shop is a meat lovers' paradise. The Pepper family has run this place for years and knows all about meat from the butcher shop. You can buy your meat in the market portion of the place or elect to order off the menu and eat it here at one of the barebones wooden tables they offer. Here you'll find steaks, burgers, surf & turf, and seafood. I usually start with a seafood appetizer (the charred drunken shrimp or the bacon wrapped scallops) and then move on to a hearty meat entrée from the dozen or so wonderful cuts they let you choose from. I either get a thick New York strip or the bone-in ribeye. A fairly priced wine list is available.

JOE'S DINER
9331 Tamiami Trail N. Suite 14, Naples, 239-254-7929
NO WEBSITE
CUISINE: American
DRINKS: No Booze

SERVING: Breakfast & Lunch
PRICE RANGE: $
Great spot for breakfast. Surly wait staff actually adds
to the "experience."

LATITUDE 26
Hyatt House Naples
1345 5th Ave S, Naples, 239-775-1000
https://www.hyatt.com/en-US/hotel/florida/hyatt-
house-naples-5th-avenue/napxn/dining
CUISINE: American/Fusion
DRINKS: Full Bar
SERVING: Lunch, & Dinner
PRICE RANGE: $$
NEIGHBORHOOD: Bonita Springs
Located in the Hyatt Hotel, causal waterfront eatery
serving modern American fare with a slight Southern
twist (but not much). Pretty standard menu for what it
is. Nothing different. Favorites: Crab cakes and Black
Grouper. The Half-chicken with Peruvian spices is
about the most interesting thing on the menu.
Vegetarian friendly.

LEE BE FISH
350 Royal Palm Dr, Marco Island, 239-389-0580
http://www.leebefish.com/
CUISINE: Seafood
DRINKS: Beer & Wine
SERVING: Lunch & Dinner
PRICE RANGE: $$$

Located on the side of **Old Marco Inn**, this seafood
eatery offers indoor and outdoor dining. These guys
not only have a fish market along with the restaurant,
but they own 2 boats that run out into the Gulf, so
their grouper and snapper dishes are always freshest.
Really quaint spot, whether you eat in or out. Menu
consists of grilled & fresh seafood. Favorites: Mahi-
Mahi and Fresh Grouper. Reservations recommended.

LOCAL
5323 Airport Pulling Rd N, Naples, 239-596-3276
www.thelocalnaples.com
CUISINE: Seafood
DRINKS: Beer & Wine Only
SERVING: Lunch & Dinner
PRICE RANGE: $$
Trendy seafood eatery offering a farm-to-table and
sea-to-table menu. Great daily specials (including
fresh local clams, shrimp, and fish tacos) and nice

wine selection. (The BBQ chicken is really good, too, as is the pecan crumble.)

M WATERFRONT GRILLE
4300 Gulf Shore Blvd N, Naples, 239-263-4421
http://mwaterfrontgrille.com/
CUISINE: American (New)/Seafood
DRINKS: Beer & Wine
SERVING: Lunch, & Dinner, Sunday Brunch
PRICE RANGE: $$$
NEIGHBORHOOD: Park Shore
Upscale waterfront eatery serving New American fare with a seafood focus. Favorites: Yellowfin Tuna and Southern Fried Calamari. Gluten-free options. Bottomless champagne Sunday Brunch. Award-winning wine list featuring over 250 wines.

MANGO'S DOCKSIDE BISTRO
760 N Collier Blvd #109, Marco Island, 239-393-2433
https://www.mangosdocksidebistro.com/
CUISINE: Seafood / Sushi / American
DRINKS: Full Bar
SERVING: Breakfast, Lunch, & Dinner
PRICE RANGE: $$
NEIGHBORHOOD: Smokehouse Bay
Spacious family-friendly spot for breakfast, lunch, dinner & cocktails in ultra-casual setting with light wood paneled walls. Has a seafood focused menu. It's in a modern building with a so-so décor, but if you're looking out at the water and the marinas, you won't mind the uninspiring surroundings. Favorites: Conch

Chowder; All American breakfast items are good;
Fish tacos and Lobster rolls. Gift shop.

MEL'S DINER
3650 Tamiami Trail N, Naples, 239-643-9898
www.melsdiners.com
CUISINE: Diner
DRINKS: Beer & Wine Only
SERVING: Breakfast, Lunch & Dinner
PRICE RANGE: $
There are several of Mel's diners in this part of
Florida, and they are all good.

Tulia

OSTERIA TULIA

466 Fifth Ave S, Naples, 239-213-2073
https://osteriatulia.com
CUISINES: Italian, Vegetarian Friendly
DRINKS: Full Bar
SERVING: Lunch & Dinner
PRICE RANGE: $$$
Located in a restored Italian farmhouse, this is
Florida's first osteria offering authentic rustic Italian

cuisine. Favorites include Chicken Parm and
Homemade Pasta specials. Excellent wine selection.

BAR TULIA
462 Fifth Ave S, Naples, 239-228-7606
https://osteriatulia.com/bar_tulia/
CUISINES: Italian, Vegetarian Friendly
DRINKS: Full Bar
SERVING: Lunch & Dinner
PRICE RANGE: $$$

THE FRENCH BRASSERIE RUSTIQUE
365 Fifth Ave S, Naples, 239-315-4019
https://thefrenchnaples.com
CUISINES: Italian (country Italian) for Osteria;
Gastropub for Bar Tulia; French country style &
bistro fare at The French
DRINKS: Full Bar
SERVING: Dinner
PRICE RANGE: $$

Inside at The French

I'm lumping these 3 places together (even though they're quite different) because they're all run by the same team. All 3 places are fun and throw off the same vibe. At Osteria, they've taken what's basically a storefront on a busy street and turned it into a contemporary restaurant featuring a menu of Italian pastas and pizzas. By gussying up the covered area outside, and adding plants and vines and drapes with sashes, they've created a much cozier and classy atmosphere. The French is much more open and brighter. Bar Tulia is packed but not unpleasantly so, cozier and busier. My favorites: the Chicken Liver Crostino to start at Osteria. The Cioppino anchored with black grouper is quite serviceable. At The French, I get the Duck Leg confit because I love the little side dish of Cassoulet that comes with it. At Bar Tulia, the menu is quite extensive, but I opt for the

Spanish Lamb Pizza or the Pork Schnitzel. Nice selection of desserts if you have room. Impressive cocktail selection. Spacious Patio seating at The French. You'll like each of these joints, or, like me, if you're here long enough, all of them.

OYSTER SOCIETY
599 S Collier Blvd, Marco Island, 239-394-3474
http://theoystersociety.com/
CUISINE: Seafood/Live/Raw Food
DRINKS: Full Bar
SERVING: Dinner
PRICE RANGE: $$$
Upscale eatery and raw bar offering a varied menu of local seafood. Inside it's dark and rather clubby. At the outside dining, the tables surround a fountain with dolphins spouting water. Both are very nice. Obviously, the oyster is king here and they have it in many varieties, up to the caviar level. They serve a

New Orleans Hot Pot (something I really love and seldom see, and they do a very good job with it here). I also love their Baked Oyster Platter (2 Rockefeller, 2 Spanish-style with Chorizo, 2 Casino style with garlic & bacon). Other Favorites: Chilean Sea Bass and Grilled Key West Shrimp. Raw bar specials. First class wine list and crafted cocktails.

RIVERWALK AT TIN CITY
1200 5th Ave S, Naples, 239-263-2734
http://www.riverwalktincity.com/
CUISINE: Seafood/Diner
DRINKS: Full Bar
SERVING: Lunch, & Dinner
PRICE RANGE: $$
NEIGHBORHOOD: Old Naples
One of many "nautical-style" seafood eateries in this area with both indoor and outdoor seating on the water where you can watch all the boat traffic going by. (There's a lot of it.) This place has a somewhat better menu than most of these types of places. And the "nautical" look is professional enough to make you think they actually hired someone to do it right, not just throw up an old net over a ceiling beam and that's it. Menu picks: Blue Crab Roll and Lobster Quesadilla. Live music.

SALE E PEPE
480 S Collier Blvd, Marco Island, 239-393-1600
www.sale-e-pepe.com.
CUISINE: Italian
DRINKS: Full bar
SERVING: Breakfast, Lunch, Dinner
PRICE RANGE: $$$$
This classy Tuscan-inspired Italian eatery, located at Marco Beach Ocean Resort, overlooks the beach affording beautiful sunset views. Seasonal menu includes authentic house-made pasta, seafood, and meats. Favorites include Smoked Gnocchi with Duck and the Calamata Olive bread. Excellent service, friendly staff.

SEA SALT
1186 Third Street S, Naples, 239-434-7258
seasaltnaples.com
CUISINE: Seafood
DRINKS: Full Bar
SERVING: Lunch & Dinner
PRICE RANGE: $$$
Famous for its emphasis on locally-sourced ingredients. Big emphasis on fish, but don't overlook the Wagyu rib eye. Great Italian wine list with some bargains.

SEVENTH SOUTH CRAFT FOOD & DRINK

849 7th Ave S, Naples, 239-231-4553
https://www.seventhsouth.com/
CUISINE: Seafood/American (New)
DRINKS: Full Bar
SERVING: Lunch- Sat & Sun/ Dinner Tues – Sun
(Closed Mondays)
PRICE RANGE: $$

Popular eatery offering a varied menu of fresh seafood and New American fare. A lively bar scene often garners more attention, but the menu is one of the best in the area and the room is sleek, modern, nothing shabby or dowdy like so many places in the area that look like they could use a coat of fresh paint. Standout food. I love the roasted oysters (bacon, cherry pepper, lemon basil); the beets & burrata salad; 3 or 4 pastas that deserve your close attention. If you can't make up your mind, fall back on the Red Grouper or the succulent Short Ribs. Wine list is top notch. Late night dining. Reservations recommended.

SHULA'S STEAK HOUSE

Hilton Hotel
5111 Tamiami Trail N, Naples, 239-430-4999
www.shulasnaples.com
CUISINE: American, Steakhouses
DRINKS: Full Bar
SERVING: Dinner
PRICE RANGE: $$$$
They have two porterhouses here (24 oz and 48 oz).
I've had them both, and I'm not proud of it, but they
WERE good.

SNOOK INN

1215 Bald Eagle Dr, Marco Island, 239-394-3313
https://snookinn.com/
CUISINE: Seafood

DRINKS: Full Bar
SERVING: Lunch, & Dinner
PRICE RANGE: $$
NEIGHBORHOOD: Marco Island
Casual waterfront seafood eatery offering beautiful views of Marco Bay from under thatched tiki huts or patio umbrellas. Great place for a drink during sunset.

Favorites: Seafood chowder; Grouper sandwiches and Mahi Mahi. Live Music most nights. Nice wine selection. Gift shop.

STAN'S IDLE HOUR
221 Goodland Dr. West, Goodland, 239-394-3041
www.stansidlehourgoodland.com/
CUISINE: Seafood
DRINKS: Full bar

SERVING: Lunch, Dinner
PRICE RANGE: $$
Dive-type bar with lots of character. Menu includes fresh seafood, burgers, and sandwiches. Weekends only until November. Live music.

SUNSET GRILLE
900 S Collier Blvd, Marco Island, 239-259-0771
www.sunsetgrilleonmarcoisland.com/
CUISINE: Pizza, American
DRINKS: Full bar
SERVING: Lunch, Dinner, Brunch
PRICE RANGE: $$
Beachside sports bar, with indoor or outdoor seating, located on Marco Island's beautiful South Beach. Menu favorites like Peel and Eat Gulf Shrimp and the Fried Shrimp Basket. A favorite spot for brunch.

TRIAD SEAFOOD

401 School Dr W, Everglades, 239-695-2662
www.triadseafoodmarketcafe.com
CUISINE: Seafood
DRINKS: Beer & Wine Only
SERVING: Lunch & Dinner; closes 6 p.m. during the week & 7 p.m. on weekends
PRICE RANGE: $$

A family owned and run eatery known for their "All You Can Eat" stone crabs. They sit right on the Barron River not far from the docks where stone crabs are brought in fresh. A screened-in patio is where you will gorge on stone crabs, eating on picnic tables overlooking the water. If it's not stone crab season (which runs from Oct. 15 to May 15), by all means don't overlook this place. They offer superior conch fritters, Key Lime Pie and other seafood. About 20 or 30 minutes east of Marco Island.

TRULUCK'S SEAFOOD, STEAK, AND CRAB HOUSE
698 4th Ave. S, Naples, 239-530-3131
www.trulucks.com
CUISINE: Seafood, Steakhouses
DRINKS: Full Bar
SERVING: Dinner
PRICE RANGE: $$$
Excellent steakhouse, but they also serve up stone crabs in season that rival anyone else's. Plush décor, just what you expect from an Expense Account Steakhouse.

USS NEMO

3745 Tamiami Trail North, Naples, 239-261-6366
https://ussnemorestaurant.com/
CUISINE: Seafood/Asian Fusion
DRINKS: Beer & Wine
SERVING: Lunch & Dinner/Dinner only on Sat &
Sun
PRICE RANGE: $$$

Upscale seafood eatery with an Asian flair. I suppose
the name derives from the porthole aquarium motif
ranged against the far wall. Very lovely décor. You're
supposed to be in an underwater restaurant. Blink
twice and you almost believe it. You can tell they put
some time & thought into it, unlike so many slapdash
décor jobs one sees in the area where no thought at all
went into it. Really pretty place. Favorites: Miso Sea
Bass with truffle risotto and Grilled Branzino. They
also have Prime Tuna prepared several ways – Asian
(pan seared Asian crust); Western style with

peppercorn crust and mushrooms; Indian style with
tandoori spices & yogurt; or the way I like it – fresh
herbs grilled simply. (Why cover up the taste of that
great tuna with all that other crap?) Also a Kids
menu. Classic desserts with a twist like the Nut &
Pear Bread Pudding. Reservations recommended.

VERDI'S AMERICAN BISTRO
241 N Collier Blvd, Marco Island, 239-394-5533
www.verdisbistro.com.
CUISINE: American, Seafood, Steakhouse
DRINKS: Beer and Wine only
SERVING: Dinner
PRICE RANGE: $$$
Comfortable bistro with good seafood and meat
selection. Menu favorites include Sautéed duck, Duck
Pot Stickers, Clam chowder, and Short Ribs.

WHERE TO SHOP

Palm-lined **Fifth Avenue South** and **Third Street South** are where you'll find the more interesting shopping opportunities in Naples. (This is the section called Old Naples or Old Town.)
You'll find sidewalk cafes, galleries, quaint little shops with all kinds of interesting merchandise, gift shops, Clothing boutiques. Parking is a pain in the ass, which is why it always makes sense to stay in one of the little hotels in this area.

THE BEACH HOUSE OF NAPLES
Waterside Shops, 5455 Tamiami Trail N, Naples, 239-598-4144
www.beachhousenaples.com
This women's boutique specializes in swimwear, resort wear, and swimming accessories. The shop also carries sandals, beach bags, hats, and cover ups.

Carries lines like Seafolly, La Perla, Trina Turk and L*Space.

LOUIS VUITTON
5415 Tamiami Trail N. #13, Naples: 239-254-0456
www.louisvuitton.com
The world-renowned leather goods supplier has a store here.

MARISSA COLLECTIONS
1167 Third St. S., Naples: 239=263-4333
www.marissacollections.com
Top designer names like Oscar de la Renta, Marc Jacobs, Blugirl, Sachin + Babi, Lanvin. Accessories, handbags, jewelry, beauty products, both men's and women's.

MIROMAR OUTLETS

10801 Corkscrew Re., Estero: 239-948-3766
Between Naples & Fort Myers
www.miromaroutlets.com/
Diesel, DKNY, Dolce & Gabbana, Gap, Nike, Gucci,
Guess, Hollister, J Crew, Kenneth Cole, Lacoste,
Oshkosh B'Gosh, Polo, Puma, Coach, Dooney and
Bourke, the Luggage Center, Pottery Barn, Chefs
Outlet, Crate and Barrel, Nautical Landing,
Restoration Hardware, Waterford crystal and
Williams-Sonoma.

OLD NAPLES SURF SHOP
1311 3rd St S, Naples, 239-262-1877
www.oldnaplessurfshop.com
This is the best surf shop in the area and has been here since 1983—the go-to shop for surf gear and clothing. The shop also sells and rents surfboards, paddleboards, skim boards, and skateboards. Great place to get souvenirs including their own logo line of T-shirts and rash guards. (The staff here leads paddleboard eco-tours, so you're in good hands when you go out there on the briny.)

PEACE, LOVE & LITTLE DONUTS
2622 Tamiami Trail, N. Naples, 239-213-0188
www.peaceloveandlittledonuts.com

If you love donuts this this shop (located in a gas station) is for you, even if you are in one of the most expensive towns on Florida's West Coast. Very creative variety of donuts. Try their key lime pie donut, or the one called Saigon cinnamon, which is really delicious. This is part of a chain that began in Pittsburgh.

TOMMY BAHAMA
1220 Third St., Naples: 239-643-6889
www.tommybahama.com
I go for the crab bisque and the coconut shrimp whenever I swing into this joint. Oops, sorry—come here for the shopping!

WILLIAM PHELPS CUSTOM JEWELER
4380 Gulf Shore Blvd. N., Naples: 239-434-2233
www.phelpsjewelers.com
He does sand castings of shells found on the beach here and then encrusts them with jewels. Lots of other

original art in here as well. They offer a free cleaning and inspection of your jewelry.

WATERSIDE SHOPS
5415 Tamiami Trail N., Naples: 239-598-1605
www.watersideshops.com/
Some of the finest names in luxury retail and fashionable lifestyle stores are set amid a lush landscape of 30,000 tropical plants and flowering shrubs, a 550-foot-long, hand-laid rock wall punctuated by cascading water, and dramatic lightning features. More than 60 shops and restaurants, as well as Saks Fifth Avenue and Nordstrom. De Beers, Hermes, Gucci, Cartier, Coach, Cache, Brooks Brothers, Ann Taylor, Lacoste, Michael Kors, Papyrus, Ralph Lauren.

WHAT TO SEE & DO

BEACHES

Naples is all about the beach, right? The most crowded tourist destination beach is off the Old Town (Fifth Avenue South, Fifth Street South).
Steer away from this area because it's overcrowded. To the north there are lots of hotels, so this too is not so great. If you go south to 18th Avenue South, this is a good place because it's less crowded, and when you go to the beach, you can walk along the sands and

peer up into the grounds of some of the more extravagant mansions of the really rich. Parking can be a hassle during peak times.

THE BAKER MUSEUM
5833 Pelican Bay Blvd., Naples: 239-597-1111. www.artisnaples.org/baker-museum
Always has something special they're exhibiting, but it's worth dropping by if you've never seen their permanent collection. It's surprisingly strong on American modernism (big names like Sheeler and Bluemner). Mexican art is represented by names like Orozco and Tamayo. Doesn't ignore local artists, either.

CORKSCREW SWAMP SANCTUARY
375 Sanctuary Rd W, Naples, 239-348-9151
http://corkscrew.audubon.org/
Open daily. Moderate admission fee good for entry over two days.
Enjoy a visit to the wilderness that dates back more than 500 years. This unique 2 ¼ mile boardwalk travels through pine flatwoods, wet prairie, around a marsh, and into a Bald Cypress forest – home to hundreds of wildlife including alligators, otters, white-tailed deer, songbirds, and turtles.

DOLPHIN EXPLORER
951 Bald Eagle Dr, Marco Island, 239-642-6899
www.dolphin-study.com
Fee & Reservations necessary.
A 30-foot catamaran powered by two 225 HP outboards crewed by a USCG Master Captain and

Mate. Boat can carry up to 28 passengers. Two drips daily (9 a.m. and 1 p.m., with each trip lasting 3 hours). Great way to observe marine life and ideal trip for photographers. This trip has been recognized by National Geographic.

FINDICTIVE CHARTERS
880 12th Ave S., Naples: 239-682-0559
https://www.findictivecharters.com/
Half-day or full-day tours available. The personable captain Michael can tailor the trip to fit your needs. Over 20 years fishing these waters.

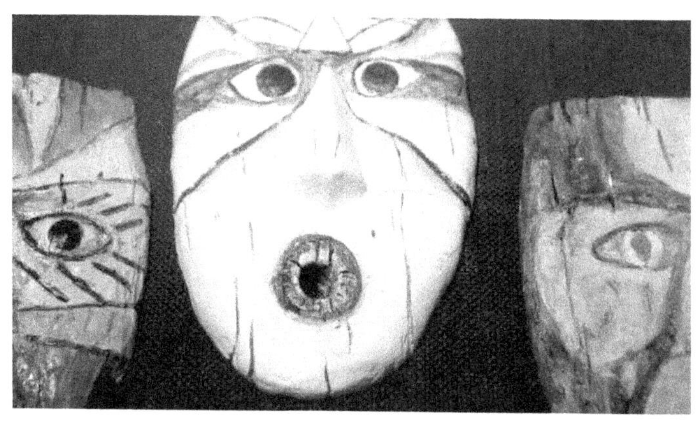

MARCO ISLAND HISTORICAL MUSEUM

180 S Heathwood Dr, Marco Island, 239-642-1440.
https://colliermuseums.com
This museum celebrates Southwest Florida's Calusa
Indians and their vanished civilization. Temporary
and traveling exhibitions trace the history of the
island. Free admission.

NAPLES BOTANICAL GARDEN

4820 Bayshore Dr., Naples: 239-643-7275
www.naplesgarden.org/
It was only as recent as 1993 that 8 residents joined to
form this attraction. Their dream was to have a world-
class botanical garden, and they have achieved their
dream. A financial gift in 2000 from the Katnick
family allowed the group to buy a 170-acre plot just
south of Old Naples.

The busy Butterfly House is a big attraction, but
they have created several themed gardens that will
keep you interested: the Asian Garden, the Florida
Garden, the Caribbean Garden, the Children's
Garden, the Brazilian Garden. Well worth your time.

NAPLES DEPOT MUSEUM

1051 5th Ave S, Naples, 239-252-8419
www.colliermuseums.com
Open Mon – Sat.
Free admission. Located in the restored **Seaboard Air Line Railway** passenger station, this museum takes visitors back to the era of the roaring '20s when traveling by rail was new and in some cases still glamorous. The museum features exhibits of Seminole dugout canoes, a mule wagon, an antique swamp buggy, restored rail cars, and interactive exhibits telling the story of a young Naples and how various transportation modes shaped the city's history. Just behind this museum is the privately-owned **Naples Train Museum** (Open Thurs – Saturday, entry fee) which features an interactive model layout and a train ride for children.
www.naplestrainmuseum.org

NAPLES ZOO AT CARIBBEAN GARDENS
1590 Goodlette-Frank Rd., Naples: 239-262-5409
https://www.napleszoo.org/
A nationally accredited zoo with animals from alligators to zebras blended into a historic botanical garden. It's basically two attractions in one. Tiger Forest, Panther Glade, and African Oasis. Wildlife presentations all day and a cruise past islands of monkeys.

OTTER MOUND PRESERVE
1831 Addison Ct, Marco Island, 239-252-2960
www.colliergov.net
This 2.45-acre preserve is located in the residential area of Marco Island. The preserve is known for the unique whelk shell terraces of the preserves signature man-made feature. Open all year. Free.

SMALLWOOD STORE

360 Mamie St, Chokoloskee, 239-695-2989
www.smallwoodstore.com
Open daily.
Small museum located on the Chokoloskee Bay.
Formerly a store for the local pioneers, this shop has
now been opened as a museum and serves as a time
capsule of Florida pioneer history. Inside the museum
is the **Tigertail Gift Shop** where you'll find books
and DVDs, authentic Seminole crafts and carvings,
alligator heads, artwork from local artists, t-shirts and
souvenirs.

SUNDAY BASH

STAN'S IDLE HOUR
221 Goodland Dr. West, Goodland, 239-394-3041
www.stansidlehourgoodland.com/

A weekly celebration featuring dancing women in feathers and live music. It's also a celebration of the Buzzard Lope Queen created by Stan. Every Sunday. Closed during summer until Oct. 1.

TENNIS
Arthur L. Allen Tennis Center
Cambier Park (across from City Hall)
735 8TH Ave. S., Naples: 239-213-3058
https://www.naplesgov.com/parksrec/page/arthur-l-allen-tennis-center
Stay away from pricey hotel tennis courts. Come down to these 12 Hydro-Grid (sub-irrigated) lighted Har-Tru (clay-like surface) courts. Meticulously maintained. Open to all. And the rates are cheap, cheap, cheap.

TIGERTAIL BEACH
Marco Island, 239-642-8414
www.tigertailbeach.net
While Marco Island is known for its mega-mansions, resorts and condo towers lining the beach, there's still this pristine, wild and beautiful wide sandy beach in a Collier County park that offers a kid-friendly water area. You may wonder how this beach escaped development. The answer: this used to be a key called Sand Dollar Island. In 2005, Hurricane Wilma deposited hundreds of tons of sand at the southern end of the island, which connected it to the mainland. Instead of walking the long route around to the connecting sandbar, try taking a shortcut by crossing the shallow lagoon. Great place for animal watching

and shelling. Kayak rentals available. Nearby café for dining.

TIN CITY

On the river in downtown Naples. Originally a fisherman's wharf (it is still used as such), it is now a large collection of shops (all indoor and air-conditioned) offering a huge array of trinkets, clothing, art, and miscellaneous.

BUSCH GARDENS TAMPA BAY

10165 N McKinley Dr., Tampa, 813-884-4386
www.buschgardens.com
ADMISSION: varies
HOURS: 10 a.m. – 6 p.m.
Busch Gardens Tampa Bay combines world-class
thrill rides, Broadway-style live entertainment and
one of North America's largest zoos in an
unforgettable adventure for the whole family. New in
209, **Iceploration** features world-class skaters, larger-
than-life puppets and even animal stars, inspiring
audiences to "explore the world" on a journey to the
four corners of the earth. Also new, the **Animal Care
Center** welcomes guests to closely observe veterinary
care and treatment at this new state-of-the-art facility,

a 335-acre 19th century African-themed animal park. It opened on March 31, 1959 as an admission-free hospitality facility for Tampa Anheuser-Busch; in addition to various beer tastings they had, a bird garden and the Stairway to the Stars which was an escalator that took guests to the roof of the brewery.

Busch Gardens continued to grow and in 1965 they opened the 29-acre **Serengeti Plains** which allowed the African wildlife to roam freely. It continued to focus on its tropical landscape, exotic animals, and amusements to draw visitors. Busch Gardens began charging admission as the entertainment became more complex, with extra fees for the thrill rides, such as the roller coasters for which Busch Gardens is now known. Currently Busch Gardens competes with other such parks in Florida and charges comparable fees. The park is operated by SeaWorld Parks & Entertainment, owned by the private equity firm The Blackstone Group. In 2011, the park hosted 4.3 million people, placing in the Top 20 of the most-visited theme parks in the US and in the Top 25 worldwide.

The Serengeti Express (a replica steam train) runs along the back end of the park and makes stops at the Nairobi, Congo and Stanleyville themed areas. The train track was recently renovated, and its tracks have been changed.

The **Skyride** transports guests between Crown Colony and Stanleyville.

MOROCCO

The park's main entrance is home to the Mystic Sheiks of Morocco brass and percussion ensemble.

Treats can be purchased at the Sultan's Sweets and the Zagora Cafe. The Moroccan Palace, a 1,200-seat indoor theatre, is located here, as well as the outdoor Marrakesh Theater. Gwazi is the major ride in this area.

GWAZI, a 105-foot, 50 mph dueling wooden roller coaster named after a mythological creature with the head of a tiger and the body of a lion opened. The dueling sides consist of a lion side and a tiger side, which cross paths seven times. In 2011 Busch Gardens replaced the original trains, which were boxy and sat four per coach. The new trains seat two per coach and should provide a smoother ride. Great Coasters International Inc. designed both the original Gwazi trains and the new Gwazi trains.

Gwazi Gliders, a small hang glider flat ride relocated from the Congo section's defunct Pygmy Village kids' area.

BIRD GARDENS

This is the original section of the park that opened back in 1959. The area for the most part remains to be mostly gardens and animal exhibits/shows. A staple attraction that once stood in this section was the brewery. However, the brewery closed in 1995 and Gwazi now sits where the brewery was located. The traditional, educational bird show is currently being replaced with a newer, more entertainment-based show, including a number of mammals.

WALKABOUT WAY

Themed as an Australian outpost, Walkabout Way opened in June of 2010. This area gives guests the chance to see and hand-feed kangaroos and wallabies. This area is home to a kookaburra, magpie geese and

Australian black swans. This experience is open to all guests 5 years of age or older.

SESAME STREET SAFARI OF FUN
Former Land of the Dragons children's section of the park. Land of the Dragons was replaced by Sesame Street Safari of Fun on March 27, 2010. It contains all the attractions from Land of the Dragons which are now re-themed. It also contains four new attractions: Telly's Jungle Jam, an interactive play area; Rosita's Djembe Fly-Away, a swing ride; Bert & Ernie's Watering hole, a water play area, and Air Grover, a children's roller coaster.

STANLEYVILLE
This section of the park is home to the park's water rides and SheiKra, which was the first and only Dive Coaster in the United States until the addition of Griffon at the sister park Busch Gardens Williamsburg. The section opened up in 1973 with the addition of the Stanley Falls Flume. The African Queen Boat Ride opened in 1977 as Busch's version of Disney's Jungle Cruise. In 1989, the African Queen Boat Ride was transformed into Tanganyika Tidal Wave with the addition of a 55-foot drop that generates a giant splash. The section remained unchanged from then until 2005, when SheiKra opened, and the surrounding area was renovated.

SHEIKRA

a 200-foot Bolliger & Mabillard floorless dive roller coaster with a 90-degree vertical drop. This is Florida's first Floorless Vertical Dive Coaster.

Stanley Falls Flume, a log flume with a 43-foot drop.

Tanganyika Tidal Wave, a 20 passenger shoot the chutes water ride with a 55-foot drop.

CONGO

Python, the park's first roller coaster. It was also Florida's first inverting roller coaster. It was removed in 2006.

This section contains two of the park's more popular rides. In November 2006, Congo underwent major renovation, including the removal of the park's classic Python roller coaster.

KUMBA, meaning roar in Swahili, is a 143-foot steel sit-down roller coaster with seven inversions. Built in 1993 by Bolliger & Mabillard, it still remains a popular ride today.

Congo River Rapids, a water ride that simulates raging whitewater rapids. The ride opened in 1982.

Ubanga Banga Bumper Cars, a bumper cars ride.

JUNGALA

Jungala is a 4-acre family attraction featuring up-close animal encounters, rope bridges to explore three stories of jungle life, and a water-play area for children. Also located in this area are two family attractions: **Jungle Flyers, a zip line** that offers three different flight patterns above the treetops of the new area, and Wild Surge, a shot tower that launches guests above a waterfall. Another attraction is Tiger Trail, which is a walkthrough with tigers where there is also a glass turret where you can look out right in the middle of the tiger enclosure. Stiltwalkers perform and interact with guests in the heart of Jungala during several parts of the day.

Jungle Fliers, a zip line ride.

The Wild Surge, a Moser family launch tower ride.

Python, an Arrow Dynamics looping coaster patterned after the original Corkscrew at Knott's Berry Farm, previously occupied the site occupied now by Jungala.

TIMBUKTU

A section themed after the malls and bazaars of Africa. The Phoenix was built in 1984 and remains a popular ride to this day. The section was renovated in 2003. Important rides added during this facelift included the Timbuktu Theater, which replaced the park's Dolphin Theater with an indoor 4-D movie theater. In 2004, Das Festhaus was transformed into the Desert Grill, and the park's family-friendly Sand Serpent wild mouse roller coaster opened, replacing the Crazy Camel flat ride.

Scorpion, a steel Schwarzkopf-designed sit-down roller coaster with one vertical loop.

Sand Serpent, a steel wild mouse roller coaster.

Phoenix, an Intamin Looping Starship themed as an Egyptian cargo vessel.

Sesame Street Film Festival 4-D a 3-D short film starring characters from Sesame Street. The film is shown in the Timbuktu Theater jointly with Pirates 4-D.

Pirates 4-D a 3-D short film about Pirates starring Leslie Nielsen. It is shown in the Timbuktu Theater jointly with Sesame Street.

Sandstorm, an orbiter ride with six arms that spins riders around. Sandstorm will be relocated to the plaza in front of the Gwazi twin coasters.

Caravan Carousel, a carousel with horses, camels, and chariots.

NAIROBI

Alligators and crocodiles can be observed here up close. In Curiosity Cavern, guests can view mammal and reptile exhibits. Visitors to Nairobi can view injured or abandoned newborns at the Nairobi Field Station Animal Nursery. The area also contains Myombe Reserve, a tropical rainforest that is home to Western Lowland Gorillas and Common Chimpanzees. The major ride here is Rhino Rally, an unpredictable off-road safari that once sent its riders down a raging river. The river portion of the attraction was eventually abandoned due to repeated vehicle breakdowns. In 2012 the Animal Care Center opened. The main train station at Busch Gardens is located at Nairobi. Another popular attraction here is the Asian Elephant exhibit, which is also featured in the Rhino Rally ride.

Rhino Rally, a Vekoma River Adventure ride,
Riders board inside modified Land Rovers through
the park's Serengeti Plain habitat, interacting with
animals.

Animal Care Center, this nearly 16,000 square-
foot attraction allows visitors the chance to view the
Busch Gardens' veterinarians at work in a new state
of the art veterinary hospital. The major visitor
aspects of the facility include a nutrition
demonstration kitchen, treatment rooms, a clinical lab
and an interactive diagnostic activity. Behind the
scenes the veterinary hospital also includes the animal
nutrition center, animal recovery and holding rooms
and vet offices. The park's former animal care center
was located behind the scenes.

CROWN COLONY PLAZA
CROWN COLONY HOUSE

Crown Colony is the smallest section of the park.
It features a restaurant, the Cheetah Hunt roller
coaster, and the Skyride station. 2009 marked the
50th anniversary of Busch Gardens, so a museum was
set up, featuring a timeline of pictures, costumes from
previous shows, and old maps of the park. It also has
a preserved Python roller coaster seat. The museum is
still there today.

Cheetah Hunt A multi-launch steel roller coaster
that opened in 2011.

Cheetah Run an animal exhibit located next to
Cheetah Hunt. It replaced the Clydesdale Hamlet.

EGYPT
Bedouin tents and authentic handicrafts and art create an Egyptian marketplace feel. Guests can visit a replica of King Tutankhamen's tomb with the excavation in progress. The primary attraction of the Egypt themed area is Montu, an inverted steel coaster.

Montu, named after the Egyptian Falcon God of War, is a 150-foot steel inverted Bolliger & Mabillard roller coaster with seven inversions.

ANIMAL EXHIBITS

CHEETAH RUN
In May 2011, Cheetah Run opened. Cheetah Run is home to Busch Gardens Tampa Bay collection of Cheetahs. There are running demonstrations and meet a keeper throughout the day. In addition, the exhibit has interactive screens with cheetah facts.

The Serengeti Plain
In 1965, the park opened its Serengeti Plain animal habitat, the first of its kind to offer animals in a free-

roaming environment. Over the years, the habitat has expanded from 29-acre to its current size of 65-acre. It is home to the Grevy's zebra, reticulated giraffe, bongo, addax, White Rhinoceros, eland, impala, ostrich, marabou stork, East African crowned crane and sacred ibis.

MYOMBE RESERVE
Giraffes at the "Edge of Africa" attraction.
A 3-acre home for six lowland gorillas and nine chimpanzees located in Nairobi, opened in 1992.

EDGE OF AFRICA
Opened in 1997, Edge of Africa is a walk-through attraction where guests can observe African animals. Among the exhibits are a Nile Crocodile, meerkats, two prides of lions, a pack of Spotted Hyenas, two hippos, vultures and a troop of lemurs.

CURIOSITY CAVERNS
This cavern attraction, formerly known as Nocturnal Mountain, contains animals such as bats, snakes, lizards, tamarins, and sugar gliders in the low-light environment. This attraction offers the true facts about the creatures inside and cracks the myths about them wide open.

REAL MUSIC SERIES
From January - March, Busch Gardens hosts a weekly concert series, which invites popular bands either in Big Bands or Pop to perform classic or contemporary songs.
Bands, Brew & BBQ

(Previously called Bud & BBQ) For the month of February, Busch Gardens hosts a series of concerts in Gwazi Field, from many classic and contemporary Country music acts; there are special culinary offerings along the walkway from the Gwazi Roller Coaster to the gate in Gwazi Field.

Viva La Musica!

In March, several Latin music acts, such as Guyacon, are hosted on the Stage in Gwazi Field. There is a similar culinary setup with special offerings for the concert days as there is for Bands, Brew & BBQ.

Summer Nights

NIGHTLIFE

Now, let's face it—people don't throng to this area of Florida for its pulsating nightlife. But there are a few things to do after the sun descends more gloriously into the Gulf waters here than most places on earth. Herewith, some suggestions:

BLUE MARTINI
MERCATO

9114 Strada Place, Naples, 239-591-2583
https://naples.bluemartini.com

The bartender here told me they feature "42 superior martinis," but I'm not quite sure what they mean by superior. (Expensive might be a better word.) I'm not big on the "specialty" cocktail craze that seems to have taken over the nation's nightlife hot spots. (Pomegranate juice in your drink?), but that's just me. A fun and lively atmosphere here. This is a part of a chain several locations around the country. Here in Naples, they offer a good mix of atmospheres, ranging from a casual patio outdoor seating where you can enjoy cocktails in the sunshine to high-energy, front and center stage where you can enjoy live entertainment and dancing until early morning. You pick. Dancing nightly. Tapas menu.

BURN BY ROCKEY PATEL

9110 Strada Place, Naples, 239-653-9013
https://www.burnbyrockypatel.com
BURN by Rocky Patel is an evolution in cigar lounges fashioned for those who enjoy fine cigars, premium spirits, delectable cuisine, trendy house music, and live entertainment. The flagship lounge opened in Naples, Florida, in 2010. (There are several others in different cities.)

DUSK
RITZ-CARLTON NAPLES

280 Vanderbilt Beach Rd, Naples, 239-598-6644
www.ritzcarlton.com
A nice, elegant lounge on the first floor of the Ritz is a nice place to relax with fancy cocktails and good sushi selections.

HAROLD'S PLACE
2555 Tamiami Trail N., Naples: 239-263-7254
www.naplesharoldsplace.com/
This little tiki bar (with mighty good burgers, I might add, as well as the grouper sandwich) is tucked behind the Quality Inn overlooking a pool, but it's a nice place to chill when the weather's good. As low key as it gets.

JOEY & MARIA'S COMEDY ITALIAN WEDDING

570 Park St, Naples, 888-562-7537
https://comedyitalianwedding.com
This is a popular dinner theater and comedy club that always packs them in.

LONDON CLUB
BELLASERA RESORT
221 9th St S, Naples, 239-231-3912
https://www.londonclubnaples.com
This is one of the better venues in the area showcasing live entertainment, they don't take reservations for music or the lounge, but they do take reservations for dinner. They have a great menu, actually. I always get the Baked Oysters Alciatore (Baby spinach, apple-smoked bacon, cream, parmesan, Pernod).

OLD NAPLES PUB
https://www.oldnaplespub.com
255 13th Ave S, Naples, 239-649-8200
Village on Venetian Bay, 4360 Gulf Shore Blvd., Naples, 239-262-2707

Soups, salads, sandwiches and entrees served for lunch and dinner in this cozy family-style pub in the heart of the fancy shopping to be enjoyed in the Third Street District. Gather around the century-old piano for a sing-along. The other location is in the Village on Venetian Bay in the Parkshore neighborhood where you'll find waterfront dining with a panoramic view.

SPAS

THE RITZ CARLTON

280 Vanderbilt Beach Rd., Naples: 239-514-6100
www.ritzcarlton.com

The three-floor Spa here was voted Best in Florida by readers of "Spa" magazine. It's no wonder why. They offer a complete range of services for body, mind and spirit.

Wraps and glows, global therapies, nail services, salon, wellness and personal training, wedding packages, aroma-reflex, facials, massage, you name it. The web site is quite detailed and has a FAQ page that will answer a lot of your questions if you've never been to a first-class spa before. **NOTE**: Spa services and facilities are only available to registered Ritz-Carlton, Naples beach and golf resort guests and Spa members. Residents and non-resort guests can use the salon and facial services in **The Salon,** located on the Lobby Level of the Spa. This little requirement sort of forces you to stay here at the Ritz, but a good way around it is to book one night here, enjoy the spa, and then move off to another property where you might rather be.

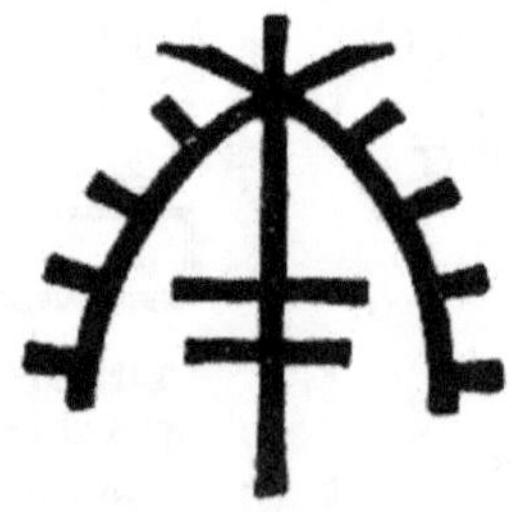

www.ingramcontent.com/pod-product-compliance
Lightning Source LLC
Chambersburg PA
CBHW061327120726
48001CB00002B/722